BLeNHeiM Palace

ISBN 978-0-9935513-1- 4
Second edition

Published by A K Associates

Dedicated
to
the
Family of Five...

with my love

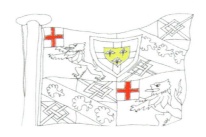

Percy
at the
Palace

(The Alternative guide to Blenheim Palace)

FLagStaFF Gate

Percy had been looking forward to visiting Blenheim Palace, but when he got there, he was a little bit worried – it was such a big place; how would a little chap like him find his way around amongst all these people?

He was just beginning to think he might go home, when someone gave his tail a gentle tug – he wasn't sure he liked this way of getting his attention – it was rather cheeky – but he looked up and saw a pretty little girl with curly hair and big blue eyes.

She looked a little mischievous and was wheeling a black bicycle with a basket and big, shiny, chrome wheels. The little girl saw Percy looking at her bicycle and said, "This is Precious, I was given her for my birthday – I ride her every day and we have some wonderful adventures together. What are you doing here?"

9

"I have come to see the Palace" said Percy, "I was so excited to come, but now that I'm here, I feel a little bit frightened; it's so BIG and I'm so SMALL and I'm afraid that I'll get lost!"

"Come with me" said the little girl, "I live here and I know my way around, I can be your guide. My name is Lady Rosemary Mildred Spencer-Churchill, but you can call me Rosie. What's your name?"

"I'm very pleased to meet you, my lady. My name is Lord Percy Piddle …but you can call me Percy."
"Very well" said Rosie and off they went!

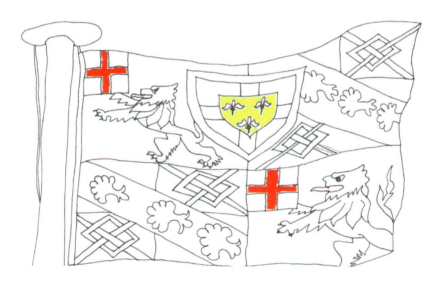

"Why is there a flag flying up there?" asked Percy pointing towards the enormous iron gate, "Does the Queen live here?"

"No, silly, the Queen lives in another Palace, in London, Buckingham Palace. The Duke of Marlborough and his family live here and, when the very fancy flag is flying, it means that they are in. When they are away, the flag of St George flies; you know, the white one with a red cross on it. It's a very good sort of flag, but it isn't as pretty as the Duke's flag!"

Rosie parked Precious up against the wall and led Percy into the Gift Shop,

"Bicycles aren't really allowed in the Palace," she explained "and neither are dogs, but I'll just say you are with me."

"This looks great" said Percy bounding towards the toys and sweets, but Rosie managed to lead him away,

THe Great Court

"Come on" said Rosie running ahead, "let's go outside."
Percy trotted after her and they found themselves in a huge
courtyard.

"Wow" said Percy, "this is e-n-o-r-m-o-u-s!"

"You haven't seen anything yet," said Rosie, "this is only the
Kitchen Courtyard so nothing too special. The kitchens used
to be over in that far corner" she said, pointing to the left of a
tall archway.

"Why were the kitchens so far from the house?" asked Percy,
"did they like to eat cold food in the old days?"

"I don't think they did, but I expect they got used to cold
food," she replied "it wasn't on purpose. When the huge fires
were lit ready to cook the food, there was always the danger
that something would go horribly wrong, and the kitchen

would catch fire and that's why they used to be so far from the main house."

The talk of food made Percy very hungry, but he thought his new friend might think him a little rude if he interrupted her to ask to go back to the café where he had spotted a nice bowl of water and a biscuit!

While Percy was dreaming about a biscuit, or even a nice

juicy bone, Rosie had run on ahead through the archway, so Percy trotted after her along the wooden cobbles, his hurried footsteps tip-tapping as he ran along. He caught up with Rosie who was staring up at the huge blue clock on top of the tower. Percy looked too – the clock seemed to be wearing a golden crown.

"What does the clock have on its head?" asked Percy pointing a paw at the tower. "Is it a crown?"

"That's not a crown, silly boy, it's a coronet. Dukes and duchesses wear coronets, not crowns. I think they are much prettier than crowns and not nearly so heavy. I don't have one because I'm not a duchess, but my mother has one – I'll show you when we go inside the Palace."

Percy was a little bit confused – surely a coronet was something he ate with ice cream – but no, thinking about it, that was a cornet! He thought that he would like to try wearing a coronet – he would have to be very careful to choose a small one that didn't slip over his eyes or else he would bump into everything. Perhaps he would keep it for special occasions… like birthdays and Christmas… and buy a lovely cloak to wear…

"Come along Percy" called Rosie as she ran off, "come and look at the Palace!"

T He PaLace

Percy looked to his left to see where Rosie was heading and, there, glowing in the bright sunshine, was Blenheim Palace! "Welcome to my home," said Lady Rosemary Mildred Spencer-Churchill solemnly.

Percy didn't quite know whether or not to believe her – did this quaint little girl with her grubby shorts and battered knees REALLY live in this Palace?

"Do you actually live in all of this?" asked Percy.

"Well, not ALL of it" answered Rosie

"Ah-ha" said Percy feeling very superior, "I thought not!"

"We only live in the rooms on the left- hand side of the Palace. We used to live in the whole lot, with all the servants, but since my mother and father opened the Palace to visitors like you, we only live in part of it. We still have lots of rooms and some of the servants do still live here, but most of the Palace is empty now – except for the furniture of course."

Percy tried to imagine what it would be like having lots of strangers visiting his house every day and decided he might not like it very much; Rosie didn't seem to mind – perhaps she was used to it, and she was certainly very friendly.

"Come on" said Lady Rosie running on ahead of the little dog, "let's go inside!"

THe Great HaLL

Percy searched for his ticket to show the doorman, but Lady Rosie simply announced, "Lord Percy Piddle is with me!" and bounded up the steps.

Gosh, perhaps she really does live here thought Percy!

Rosie stepped through the little storm door and into the Palace – Percy had very little legs so he had to be helped over the step by Archie, the Head Guide.

"Come on young man" he said, "we don't want you to fall flat on your face!"

Percy felt very, very small when he looked around the Great Hall. It was the biggest room he had ever seen and on the ceiling was a beautiful painting. It hurt his neck to look up at it.

"How did that get up there?" asked Percy, "They must have had very tall ladders or very long paint brushes in those days!"

"Oh Percy," said Rosie laughing, "You are funny. The artist put up lots of scaffolding – like you see today when the roof of a house is being built. Once the scaffolding had been put up, he could climb to the top of it, lie on his back, and start painting. He must have looked very strange when he had finished for the day. He would have been covered in paint!"

Percy didn't know quite what to say to that, but then he caught sight of something in a case which looked very interesting.

"What's that Rosie?" asked Percy pointing at the glass case.

"That's the Palace key" she replied "do you want to have a closer look?"

"Ooo, yes please" he said bouncing up and down a bit with his tail wagging. "What's that on top of it?"

"That's another coronet" said Rosie "like the one we saw on the clock. Do you remember?"

"Oh yes, of course," said Percy, "Where's the lock?"

"Turn around and look at the door. You can see the lock there. It's meant to be the same

shape as a map of Poland and the key fits in that little door. I'll ask Archie to show us."

"Where is Poland?" asked Percy who was very young and didn't know a lot about other countries.

"It's a country which is quite a long way away, but don't worry about that now, we can look it up later" said Lady Rosie trying to quickly change the subject. "Let's see if Archie will show us how it works."

Archie was a very kind man and, after looking around him to make sure there was no-one else looking, he said, "C'mon, quickly or you'll get me into trouble." With that, he scooped Percy up under his arm and lifted him up so that he could tap on the lock to open it up before popping the key inside.

"Wow" said Percy as he took the key out again – although he wasn't sure he liked being up quite so high. Archie gave him a little tickle under his chin before setting him back down on the stone floor and Percy took the opportunity to give him a quick lick on the nose. He had made another friend.

20

"Where to now?" asked Percy, he was beginning to enjoy himself – the people here were very friendly – he couldn't think what he had been so worried about.

"Let's go down here" said Rosie, I've got something funny to show you," and with that, she ran off down a corridor lined with marble statues. Percy was so busy trying to look up at the statues that he quickly lost sight of his guide,

"Rosie" he called in a bit of a panic "where are you?" Suddenly the Palace felt big and scary again.

"Here I am Percy," she called, "do keep up. It's almost lunch time and I daren't be late. Mr Taylor, the butler, always sounds the gong at one o'clock and if I'm not sitting at the table, hands washed and hair brushed, then I won't be allowed out for a week!"

Percy didn't want his new friend to get into trouble because of him, so he ran along as fast as his little legs would carry him and soon they reached a very pretty bedroom.

The Bedroom

"How strange to have a bedroom downstairs like this" said Percy. He was sure this house was too big to be a bungalow, so why would there be a bedroom here he wondered?

"Lots of Palaces and big houses like this have bedrooms on this floor," said Rosie," in fact, all the smartest rooms are down here – and the best rooms have the biggest windows!"

"Oh look, someone has left a giant teacup beside the bed," said Percy "what a strange thing to do."

Rosie looked at Percy and smiled, "it may look like a teacup," she laughed, "but I can assure you it isn't. It's a chamber pot, a potty!"

"A what?" said Percy blushing slightly.

"A potty!" said Lady Rosie "When my parents came to live in the Palace many, many years ago, there was only one bathroom so everyone had one of those in case they needed the lavvy in the night. I think they are rather pretty – they have an 'M' for Marlborough on them. If you lived here, you would have to have one with a 'P' for Percy on it" she laughed.

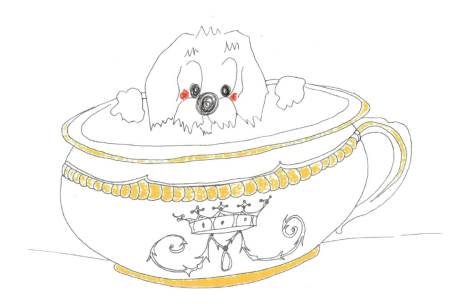

"The 'lavvy'?" asked Percy "What's that?"

"You know - a lavatory - a toilet – a loo!"
Percy looked rather put out – he was still only a puppy really, but he was very proud of the fact that he had been dry at

night for a very long time and didn't need a lavvy, a loo, or a toilet!

"There's no need to pull a face," said Rosie – "believe me, when you live in a great big house like this and the only bathroom is 5 minutes away, there are times when you are very glad of a potty!"

Percy thought that it was perhaps time to move on from this subject and as he looked around him, he noticed a painting of a very pretty little girl.
"Who is that?" he asked, "is she one of your relations?"

"**She**?" giggled Rosie, "That is very much a **he** - and a very important 'he' at that." Rosie suddenly stopped laughing, stood up very straight, put her shoulders back and proclaimed,

"That little boy was my grandfather's cousin. His name was Winston, Winston Churchill and he was born here and went on to become the Prime Minister of this country – twice! He was a very special man."

As she spoke, Rosie had become very serious but Percy still didn't believe that he was looking at a picture of a boy! Perhaps Rosie had made a mistake.

"Are you sure that's a boy?" asked Percy "why on earth is he wearing a frilly collar and ringlets? You wouldn't catch me with my hair in ringlets!"

"I hadn't really thought about it before," said Rosie "I do remember my governess telling me once that Victorian boys used to wear frilly smocks until they were five years old and that was also when they had their hair cut for the first time. That happened to Winston. Look, you can see his curls on the bedstead. They are over 100 years old!"

"Goodness me!" said Percy, "how very peculiar. Fancy keeping someone's hair for all that time!"

"It's not so very unusual," said Rosie "my parents have still got some of my baby curls and I would imagine that your mummy and daddy have kept some of yours too? Actually," said Rosie, "what am I saying? It would be a lot more unusual if **your** parents had kept some! You're a dog."

With that, the two friends ran out of the bedroom, and found themselves back in the corridor with the statues.

"Come on" said Rosie "follow me" and off she went.

T**HE** G**REEN** D**RAWING** R**OOM**

Percy only just managed to keep up; Rosie was much taller than him and had very long legs compared to his very short ones. They passed lots of portraits – some of stern old Dukes and some of smiling pretty, Duchesses, and as they ran, Rosie pointed out huge paintings of her parents and grandparents, great-grandparents and great-great grandparents.

Eventually, Rosie came to a halt in a very pretty room with a beautiful light hanging from the ceiling.

"This is the **Green** Drawing Room" said Rosie "There are lots more pictures of my ancestors in here. Some of them lived here hundreds of years ago and the lady on the wall by the door dressed in black is Sarah, the first Duchess of Marlborough and she was here when the Palace was being built."

"Goodness" said Percy "you are lucky to have so many old family photographs – and such big ones too!"

"They're not photographs, silly. Cameras hadn't been invented in those days. They are paintings. But yes, we're very lucky to have them. It makes me feel as though I know them all.

"That great big light must take a lot of polishing. It's very pretty" said Percy,
"Yes" said Rosie "it does. The proper name for it is a 'chandelier' and when it was first put here, it used to have candles in it and someone had the job of lighting them each day and then snuffing them out again when everyone had gone to bed."

"They must have needed a lot of puff" said Percy "I can't even manage to blow out the candles on my birthday cake" said Percy in admiration.

"I don't think they blew them out" said Rosie, picturing a group of footmen huffing and puffing, "they used to use a special thing that looked like a pointed hood at the end of a long stick. It would have been a lot quicker…and would have saved the room from getting covered in spit!" she laughed.

Percy laughed too. What a strange day this was becoming. When he arrived at Blenheim Palace he hadn't expected to make a new friend – let alone a very pretty one who talked about potties and spit!

THe Red DraWiNg RooM

"Come in here" said Rosie "this is one of my favourite rooms. It's the **Red** Drawing Room this time."

Percy found himself in another beautiful room. It had a very fancy ceiling with lots of gold everywhere.

"Is that real gold?" asked Percy

"I don't think so" said Rosie "the carvings are made from wood and then covered in gold leaf."

"Gold leaves?" asked Percy "Like you find in the autumn when they fall off the trees? Gosh!"

"You are funny" said Rosie fondly "It's just very, very thin gold which comes in a kind of book but, instead of being made of paper, the pages are made of very thin gold."

"Wow!" said Percy "That's amazing. Imagine, pages made of gold..." and off he went into a little daydream about being a pirate and discovering a hoard of buried books and all the pages were made of gold...

"Percy. Are you listening to me?" asked Rosie a little crossly.

"Yes, of course I am" said Percy leaving his daydream behind "you were talking about that great big picture at the end of the room..." he said hopefully.
"Yes, as I was saying, the little boy in the middle of the picture is my father, Bert, and he grew up to be the 10th Duke. The artist was very cross with him because he wouldn't keep still while he was being painted and eventually he fell off a chair and broke his leg so the painting took ages to finish."

Percy had to fight back a smile – "so that's where Rosie gets her mischievous streak from" he thought.

"I think I would have liked the young Bert," said Percy "but I feel sorry for him having to wear such odd looking clothes!"

Lady Rosie looked a little bit cross as Percy said that, but then she laughed. "Don't you worry, he didn't wear them for long

– he was too busy having fun playing in the garden with his little brother."

Percy bit his tongue this time and managed not to say that he thought the other child in the picture was a little girl. How strange people were in the old days.

Rosie went on, but, before he followed her, Percy, who was beginning to feel a little bit weary, caught sight of the very thing for a tired sausage dog. It was a very l-o-n-g sofa. Percy had a very l-o-n-g body... before he knew it, Percy had sneaked under the red rope which kept visitors at bay, jumped up onto the sofa, rolled onto his back, stretched out, yawned and was fast asleep.

"Zzzzzzzzzz..." Percy was having a very strange dream where he was chasing a little girl with blue eyes and curly hair but when he called her, she turned into a little boy called Bert and he rode away on a black bicycle with shiny chrome wheels...

"Percy Piddle, WAKE UP! What are you doing on that sofa?" said a familiar voice. It was Archie doing his rounds. "We're going to open the Palace shortly. We don't want the visitors

to think you're part of the furniture. What have you done
with Lady Rosemary?"

"I'm here" said Rosie "I was talking about the next room
when I realised I'd lost him. Are you feeling alright Percy?

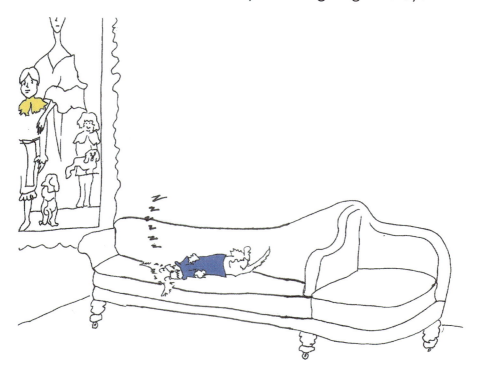

And what are you doing on that sofa? We'll be in trouble if
my mother catches us. It's over a hundred years old and no,
it wasn't designed as a bed for sausage dogs! It was made
like that so that a boy and a girl could sit at each end and
someone else, a 'chaperone' could sit on that small seat to

keep an eye on them and make sure that they didn't do anything soppy like hold hands. Yuuuuuuukkkk!"

"I'm fine now that I've had a little rest" said Percy "there's so much to see...and I am beginning to feel a little peckish..."

"Never mind about that now" said Rosie "come and look at the desk in the **Green** Writing Room"

Tₕₑ Gᵣₑₑₙ Wᵣᵢₜᵢₙg Rₒₒₘ

The twosome trotted off together into another beautiful room. It wasn't quite as big as the last one, but it had lots of interesting things in it and lots of pictures on the walls. Rosie wasn't looking at the walls, she was pointing at the desk at the far side of the room. Percy didn't think it looked much like a desk; no computer, no books, no files, no clutter.

"I was saying earlier – before I realised that I'd lost you – that hundreds of years ago, people used to write letters all the time and before proper pens were invented, they used to use sharpened goose feathers dipped in ink to write with."

"Really" said Percy "how peculiar." Percy was thinking rather guiltily that he didn't take much care with his writing at the best of times; goodness knows what it would look like if he had to use a scratchy old feather!

"Yes. It was peculiar" agreed Rosie "there used to be lots of desks everywhere throughout the Palace so that guests could quickly write a note and it was someone's job to make sure that there was always paper, ink, wax..."

"Just a minute" interrupted Percy "why would you need wax to write a letter? Do you mean wax crayons in case you wanted to draw a picture?"

"Oh Percy, you do have some peculiar ideas. No you wouldn't use the wax to draw with. In those days, people didn't put their letters in envelopes, so they would fold the letter, melt some wax and then drop some of the melted wax onto the edges to seal it. You certainly wouldn't be able to steam the letter open to have a peep!"

"Tee hee" giggled Percy as if such an idea would ever cross a naughty little dog's mind!

"I think you will like the next room," said Rosie giving Percy's tail a gentle tug to get his attention.

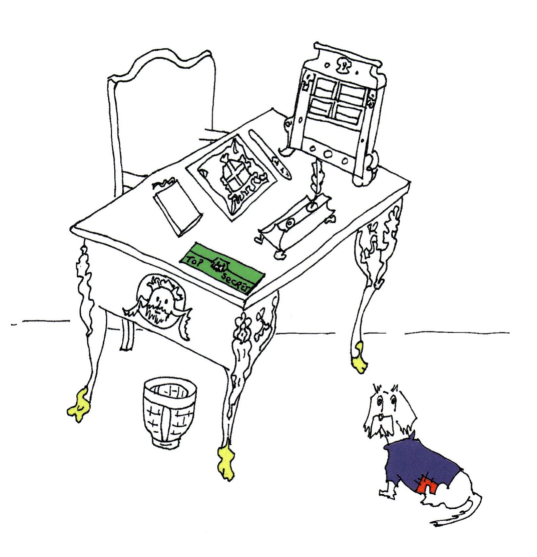

THe SaLooN

"What an echoey room!" said Percy trotting along behind Lady Rosie.

"Yes, it is isn't it" agreed Rosie "it is called 'The Saloon' and it's where my father, the Duke, has his Christmas dinner. It's a very old table and it can stretch so that it's even longer than it is now. You can sit 42 people around it – but the Butler tells me that fitting in the side plates is a bit of a squash!" Lady Rosie laughed, "I daresay you could get even more of your family and friends around it as you would only need a bowl!"

She seemed to find this very funny and laughed and laughed until the tears began streaming from her eyes and every now and again, she gave a very unladylike snort.

Percy looked a little bit cross – he didn't like to be laughed at – but he soon forgot to be cross when he heard Lady Rosie describing the wonderful food that the older members of the family ate on Christmas Day. There was turkey and ham, beef and lamb, chicken, salmon and lobster; cherries and ice cream… Percy was licking his lips and, it has to be said, dribbling a little, when he heard Lady Rosie say sadly,

"Of course that's not what I get. I still have to have my dinner in the Nursery with Nanny. It's just not fair! My dinner's not nearly as exciting and Nanny still makes me go to bed at 7 o' clock even though it's Christmas Day and my brothers

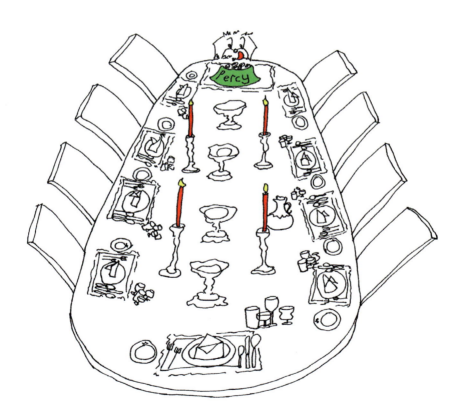

can stay up. When I'm a grown up, I will stay up as **late** as I please and eat **what** I please, **when** I please."

Rosie looked very cross for a moment so Percy stood very still and very silent – something which was actually very difficult for a very fidgety young pup… Luckily, Rosie's bad mood left her as quickly as it had come on and she skipped off to the next room cheerfully humming a Christmas carol.

The Three State Rooms

"This is the First State Room" she announced, "followed by the Second and Third State Rooms."

Percy smiled to himself for a moment; they were very unimaginative names for such beautiful golden, sparkling rooms.

"Can you see the crib there?" asked Lady Rosie "that was given to my grandmother by her mother and my father used to sleep in it when he was a baby."

This time, it was Percy who had a little laugh to himself.

"Why are you smiling?" asked Lady Rosie a little stiffly.

"The reason I'm smiling," said Percy in a very patient manner, "is that I was just thinking of your father as a baby, in the crib, and someone giving the crib a good hard push. He would fall plop, onto the floor!"

41

"Oh no he wouldn't" replied Rosie "his Nanny or Nursemaid would have made sure of that – there would have been someone keeping an eye

on him all the time. He was very precious, he was born to be the next Duke and had his own Butler and Valet and Chef and, and **everything**!"

The next room, the Second State Room was just as beautiful as the First and had a very interesting picture on the wall.

"Look! There's a dog" said Percy wagging his tail round and round in his excitement and pointing at an enormous picture on the far wall. "Why is he chasing that horse? Only very naughty dogs chase horses!" said Percy in a very stern voice.

"I don't think the dog is chasing the horse, he's just trying to keep up with it. He belonged to the man on the horse and used to go into battle with him," explained Lady Rosie "he was a very brave dog."

"What was his name?" asked Percy

"We don't know" said Rosie wistfully, "I think it should be something rather grand, like Albert the Adventurous"

"Or Bruno the Brave" said Percy

"Or Victor the Valiant" said Lady Rosie

"Hector the Hero" said Percy

"Godfrey the Great" said Rosie

"Ludovic the Loyal" said Percy

"Tosca the Terrible" said Rosie

"Norbert the Noble" said Percy

"Percy the Pickle" said Rosie laughing

"…or we could just call him Bob!" said Percy firmly as he trotted off towards the next room!

The Third State Room looked very much like the two rooms

which had gone before, but Percy was far too polite to say so. He looked around him at all the beautiful furniture while Rosie pointed out a statue of the very, very first Duke of Marlborough.

"Oh look! The Duke has kept his long curly hair. Why

wasn't his cut when he was five years old like the little boy we saw earlier? asked Percy

"That's not his hair" said Rosie a little impatiently, "he's wearing a wig!"

"Why," asked Percy, "was he bald?"

"No, it was very fashionable to wear a wig and only very rich and important people could afford to wear them and they used to put powder on them too so that they all looked as though they had grey hair. They were a funny lot!"

Suddenly Percy heard a ringing in his ears. He shook his head from side to side and rubbed his ear along the red carpet.

"What on earth are you doing now?" asked a very puzzled Rosie "do you have an itchy ear?"

"No, it's just that I seem to have a ringing in my ears and I'm trying to get rid of it"

"Percy Piddle are you serious? That's the clock behind you chiming to tell us that it's half past twelve – which means we must get a move on or else I will be late for lunch and I told you before what will happen to me if I'm late!"

Percy felt a bit silly, he got up from the floor very slowly and tried to make it look as though he always threw himself on the floor while furiously rubbing his head.

He looked up to see where the chimes had come from, but was too tiny to see, so he did the first thing that he thought of, and that was to stand up on his back legs and hold up his front paws for Rosie to pick him up so that he could look at the beautiful gold clock.

"Goodness me you're far heavier than you look" said Rosie struggling to pick Percy up. "Can you see the clock now? I don't think I can hold you up for much longer…"

Percy looked up and saw a marvellous clock covered with tiny golden statues of tiny golden people and then he caught sight of a sun swinging from side to side and the sun had a face and it was all making the most wonderful, calming, gentle tick-tocking sound…

"Percy! Wake up" shouted Lady Rosie "I'm about to drop you. Watching the pendulum must have sent you to sleep" she laughed.

Percy jumped down out of Rosie's arms and had a great big stretch and a great big yawn and thought longingly of the long red sofa in the Red Drawing Room. A little nap was just what he needed…a little nap and some food!

"Come on. One last room to go. I think you will like this one."

THE LONG LIBRARY

Percy trotted on ahead of Lady Rosie this time. What must she think of him, falling asleep in her arms like that? He was very lucky that Rosie had managed not to drop him; he was quite a small dog, but then she was quite a small girl – but a very strong and kind one - he could tell.

"This is the Long Library" announced Lady Rosie in a very solemn voice "because it is very long…and it is full of books!"

Percy looked around him – it was indeed full of books – big books, little books, old books, new books, every type of book. "Some of them are hundreds of years old" said Lady Rosie "and some of them are very new, but they are all very interesting"

"How do you know? Have you read them all?" asked Percy in great admiration and wonder.

"Wellll....not exactly all of them...but come along I want to show you something else" she said, quickly changing the subject. Percy was very relieved...he liked books...very much...but he found he much preferred smaller, thinner ones, preferably with lots of pictures... lots of words could be very, very confusing for a small dog...

Lady Rosie ran towards the centre of the room and stopped

beside a beautiful bow window and pointed at the clothes on show there. She explained that some of them were uniforms which had been worn by Blenheim servants over a hundred years ago, but the long, red robes had been worn by Lady Rosie's grandparents when they went to see the King being crowned.

"But we haven't got a King" said Percy then, standing very still and stretching to his full height (which wasn't very full at all..) he solemnly announced, "we have a Queen. Her majesty Queen Elizabeth" and with that, he put one of his front paws on his chest in a doggy salute.

Unfortunately, Percy lost his balance, fell awkwardly and found himself in the folds of a long, red cloak. His head couldn't be seen, but Lady Rosie could just see his tail poking out – but there was definitely no wagging going on!

"Percy! Stop playing the fool. Come out of there at once before we both get into trouble" and with that, Lady Rosie grabbed both of Percy's back legs and yanked him firmly out of the family robe.

"I know we have a Queen – I was about to tell you that my grandparents had worn these robes and then they were handed down to my parents who wore them years and years later when they went to London to see Queen Elizabeth being crowned."

Percy thought it was very strange that Rosie's parents lived in a great big Palace, but wore hand-me-downs…you would think they could afford to buy a nice new outfit to wear to London to see the Queen.

If Percy was ever invited to see the Queen, he would wear his best top hat and he would also wear a smart jacket with long tails and a very smart dickie bow and…

"Percy, what on earth are you doing standing there day-dreaming? Come here, I want to show you something. What can you see in there?"

Lady Rosie was standing next to a glass cabinet and, when he stood on tiptoe, Percy could just see three red crowns – a big one, a medium sized one and a teeny-tiny one. It reminded him a little bit of the story of the Three Bears – perhaps they had visited Blenheim Palace too…?

"I can see three crowns" said Percy

"No you can't" said Lady Rosie

"Yes I can" said Percy doing a quick recount as sometimes his counting could be a little bit wobbly

"No" said Lady Rosie "You can see two coronets and a cap!"

Well, the cap wasn't like any cap Percy had ever seen before, but Rosie explained that it had belonged to Queen Ann, a Queen who had lived hundreds of years ago and who had been a very good friend to Rosie's great ancestor, the First Duke of Marlborough.

"I've already explained to you about what a Duke and Duchess wear – do you remember what these special hats are called?"

"Let me think" said Percy "…I KNOW!" he shouted in great excitement "They are called…cornets!"
Rosie buried her head in her hands and shook her head in despair.

"They are NOT called 'cornets' as I said before, a cornet is something you put your ice-cream in. These are called C-O-R-O-N-E-T-S. CORONETS!"

As if shouting at Percy hadn't been enough, Lady Rosie had actually stamped her foot in frustration...the day was beginning to go horribly wrong... then suddenly, Lady Rosie began to laugh; she laughed and laughed and wiped a tear from her eye and then managed to gulp down a very UN-ladylike snort.

"Whatever's the matter?" asked Percy wondering if he should call for help.

"Well, they didn't put ice-cream in their coronets" Rosie managed to say in between some spectacular snorts and giggles, "but they had to wait in their seats for hours and hours before the Queen was crowned so they did put their sandwiches in their coronets so that they didn't faint from hunger. In fact, it wouldn't surprise me if one or two of them didn't sneak a potty under their robes too..."

Percy said he would rather not think about the potty aspect of the day, but the mention of sandwiches was making him hungry again.

"That reminds me" said Rosie "it really is time for me to go. Taylor will sound the gong in a few minutes and I'll be for it if I'm late again this week."

With that, Lady Rosie trotted off again with an occasional snort as she thought of her parents with their sandwiches in their coronets. It was a good job they had eaten their sandwiches before they had to put their coronets on their heads!

Percy followed Lady Rosie down the rest of the Long Library, past an enormous piano looking thing and out through one of the biggest doors Percy had ever seen. They ran on along the colonnades where they found themselves high above the Courtyard.
"Oh no" said Percy pointing down into the Great Court where a young man was standing with Rosie's bicycle, "someone has taken Precious!"

"Oh don't worry," she laughed, "that's Ron Petch, one of our gardeners. I'm afraid I do sometimes leave Precious behind

and Mr Petch often finds her, then he finds me and then Precious and I go off on another adventure.

Come on, let's go down and you can jump in the basket and I'll take you back to where I found you. We'll have to watch out for all these visitors and make sure we don't run any of them over, or else I will really be in trouble!"

Percy had never ridden a bicycle before – his legs were just too short to reach the pedals, but he liked the idea of being a passenger and not having to do any of the hard work!

"Woo hoo!" he shrieked as they whizzed through the Clock Arch "This is great fun!"

Before he knew it, Percy and Rosie had reached the end of their journey.

"Well my Lord Percy Piddle. It has been a great pleasure to meet you" said Lady Rosie shaking Percy by the paw.

"It has been a great pleasure to meet you too my Lady Rosemary Mildred Spencer-Churchill" said Percy and then he sighed.

"What is it?" asked Rosie giving Percy a little pat on the head.

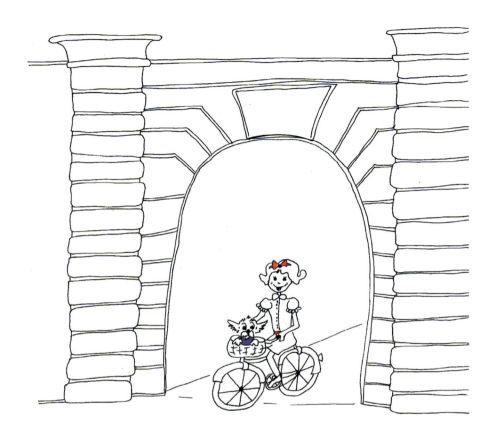

"Well, I've had such a wonderful day. I've really enjoyed looking at your beautiful home and I'm a little bit sad that my visit has come to an end" sniffed Percy rather mournfully.

"But that doesn't matter! You will come again won't you? I've only shown you the Palace" said Rosie "there's so much

more I need to show you. I thought that next time, we could get Nanny to pack a picnic for us and we'll row across to the Grand Bridge and we can have our picnic in one of the rooms which isn't full of water! What do you think?"
"What do I think?" said Percy "I think that's a great idea!" and with that, he stood on his hind legs, gave Lady Rosie a great big lick on the nose and trotted off home for lunch!

Percy lives very happily with his human family, his best doggy friends Albert and Ludo, 5 chickens, a cockerel and assorted cats. He is a very cheeky young sausage dog and gives everyone he lives with an awful lot of pleasure...except when he is naughty of course and disappears off on an adventure without telling anyone!

Lady Rosie really did live at the Palace – until 1953 when, after being a maid of honour at the coronation of Queen Elizabeth, she left to marry and she became a very grown up Lady Rosemary Muir – but she still has very twinkly eyes and a wicked sense of fun!

...and she really did have a bicycle called Precious...

Ron Petch was a gardener at the Palace from 1938, who left Blenheim to fight in World War II and then thankfully returned.

Archie looked after all the people who visited Blenheim Palace in the days when the Palace was only open a few days a week and it cost the princely sum of 2/6d (12.5p) to get in!

As for Mr Taylor, he was the butler at Blenheim from the mid-1930s until after World War II – and he never did sound the gong for lunch a moment after 1 o'clock – even to please Lady Rosie!

I do hope you have enjoyed reading about the first of Percy's visits to Blenheim Palace.

Look out for Percy's other adventures:

Percy in Peril

Percy's picnic nearly ends badly when he discovers that hungry Old Pike still lives in the murky waters of the Lake

Percy and the Present

Percy spends Christmas with Lady Rosie and her family

Percy's Path (absolutely **NOT** to scale)

The bit Where Lady Rosie Lives

Kitchen Court

Great Court